"The waters of **Baptism**

are indeed

faithful and *trustworthy*,

for they *flow* with the

power of **Christ's love**,

the *source* of our assurance

in the *journey of life*."

Pope Francis (Lumen Fidei, no. 42)

My Baptism

REMEMBRANCE BOOK

Mary Martha Moss, FSP

Illustrations by Veronica Walsh

Pauline
BOOKS & MEDIA
Boston

Dedicated to my two grandnieces,
Brenly Elizabeth and Charley Jane Moss.
May Jesus always shine in your hearts!

I would like to express my deep gratitude and appreciation
to Marlyn Evangelina Monge, FSP for her loving dedication
in the developmental editing of this beautiful edition.
I would also like to say a hearty "thank you!" to the sisters and staff
(you know who you are!)
of the fifteen Pauline Books & Media Centers in the U.S. and Canada
who contributed with suggestions
and support toward the writing of this book.
Together with all of you,
I thank God for this work of love and prayer!

Cover and book design by Mary Joseph Peterson, FSP

Cover art and illustrations by Veronica Walsh

Excerpt from *Lumen Fidei* © 2013 Libreria Editrice Vaticana, Vatican City. Used with permission.

ISBN 0-81981-4929-4

Published by Pauline Books & Media, 50 Saint Pauls Avenue, Boston, MA 02130-3491

Printed in Korea

MBDR SIPSKOGUNKYO10-8028 4929-8

www.pauline.org

Pauline Books & Media is the publishing house of the Daughters of St. Paul, an international congregation of women religious serving the Church with the communications media.

123456789   18 17 16 15 14

Contents

Remembrance of My Baptism   1

Stories from the Bible   19

My Prayers   35

Growing Up   43

Remembrance of My Baptism

My name is _____

This name was chosen for me by _____

My name was chosen for me because _____

_____

I was born

Date _____

Time _____

Weight _____ Length _____

City, State/Province, Country _____

I received the sacrament of Baptism on _____

I was baptized by (priest or deacon) _____

My Baptism took place in the Church of _____

I was baptized (city, state/province, country) _____

_____

My godparents are _____

Family and Friends

On the day of your Baptism, something wonderful happened! You became part of God's loving family and a member of the Church. You did not do this alone. There were others there with you to celebrate that very important day. These are the family and friends who were with you at your Baptism . . .

Messages, prayers, and words of wisdom from family and friends on my Baptism day

Did you know?

Your family and friends pray for you and want the best for you. It is important for you to pray for your family and friends. Just as you need prayers and help, they too need prayers and help. There are many ways that you can be of help to others. What are some of the ways that you think you can help others?

Messages from my godparents

Did you know?

Your godparents have a special job. Not only were they there at your Baptism, they also promised to pray for you and help you learn more about your faith. Ask your godparents to talk to you about God. You can ask them to read with you a story from the Bible! You can ask them to help you learn a prayer by heart. You can even ask them to tell you what they like the best about going to Church. Your godparents want to help you learn more about God!

Memories from the day of my Baptism

My baptismal clothes symbolize that I "put on Christ" from this day forward. This is what they looked like

Other memories of how my family celebrated my baptismal day

Food, decorations, other things that happened on that special day

_____

_____

_____

_____

_____

_____

_____

_____

Gifts I received and those who gave them

Firsts
and
Favorites

As you continued to grow, many things happened that are worth remembering. God has watched you grow. God loves you very much!

My first Christmas _____

My first Easter _____

My first birthday _____

My first tooth _____

Rolling over _____

Sitting up _____

Crawling _____

First step _____

First word _____

Favorite toy _____

Favorite place in the house _____

Other favorite things _____

_____

_____

_____

God's Family

My Family

Your own family is part of the great family of God. Think of all the people you love and write their names below.

Me

My Parents

My Brothers and Sisters

My Grandparents

My Aunts and Uncles

My Cousins

Other Relatives

You are very blessed. Because you are baptized, you are a member of God's family, too!

On the Day
You Were Baptized

The day of your Baptism was a very special day. God loves you and he wants you to be his child forever. Your Baptism may have been celebrated during the Mass. It may have been in a special ceremony in the church or even in another place. Wherever it was celebrated, your family and friends were glad to be there with you. The day of your Baptism was the day you became a child of God and a member of the Church.

Welcomed with joy

On the day of your Baptism, the priest or deacon welcomed you, your family, and friends at the door of the church with great joy. He asked, "What is this child's name?" Your name is important. God knows you and calls you by your name. At your Baptism, you were called by your name for the first time in church! Your parents promised to teach you about God and how to follow Jesus. Then the priest or deacon made the sign of the cross on your forehead. Being marked by the sign of the cross means that you were claimed by Jesus.

Listening to God's word

After that someone read from God's holy book, the Bible. We are God's people and the Bible tells God's story. This is your story, too. It's about all of God's family. At your Baptism you became a member of God's big family. Reading and listening to the Bible will help you make good choices.

Saying "yes" to God

It is likely one or both of your parents spoke for you. They said that you wanted to belong totally to God. They spoke up for you because, if you were just a baby, you could not speak for yourself. They said "yes" to God for you! They said "no" to all that is not of God. After that, they prayed an Act of Faith. This prayer expresses their faith that God will take care of you and live in your heart. God lives inside every person who has faith in him. God is very happy to live inside you. There is an Act of Faith you can pray on page 39.

A special gift

The priest or deacon then poured blessed water on your forehead three times. He poured the water three times because you were baptized in the name of the Father, the Son, and the Holy Spirit.

When you were baptized something amazing happened. You were given a very special gift! You started your life with God! The Holy Spirit made a home inside you! Baptism is a very powerful gift. You belong to God forever now.

After you were baptized with water, the priest or deacon blessed you with holy oil. You were given white clothes and a lit candle. The candle was lit from the flame of the big Easter candle. Your godparents held it for you. It symbolized that God's light was now inside you.

At the end of your Baptism, the priest or deacon prayed a special blessing over you, your parents, and your godparents. These prayers asked God to give you strength. The celebrant then blessed you to help you as you started out as a follower of Jesus.

Each day you can pray to ask God to help you live the faith God gave you at Baptism. Prayers in the morning and evening will help you do that! You can find some common prayers beginning on page 35. Going to Mass each Sunday will help you, too.

Symbols of Baptism

There are many symbols in Baptism. Here is an explanation of some of them. Whenever you see these symbols they can remind you of your Baptism!

The door to the church

Baptism begins at the door of the church. This is because Baptism is the "door" to the other sacraments. It is the door to God's home. When you went through the door of Baptism, you became a child of God and a part of God's family forever. You can pray to God as "our Father."

The water

Water is a powerful symbol. The water at Baptism is a symbol of life, growth, cleansing, and rising to eternal life. All living things need water to live and grow! We need the waters of Baptism to live and grow fully in God. Water is used for cleansing and healing. In Baptism you were cleansed of original sin.

In addition to giving us life, growth, cleansing, and healing, water can also be very powerful. Think of fierce storms and giant ocean waves crashing on the shore. Water can even cause death. In Baptism you were united to Jesus's life, death, and resurrection. Jesus promises to be with you always. He walks with you every step of the way until you reach eternal life.

Water was used to baptize you in the name of the Father, the Son, and the Holy Spirit. Before the water was poured over your head, the priest or deacon said a special prayer over it. That prayer asked the Holy Spirit to give all who are baptized in Christ eternal life. Because you were baptized you share in Christ's eternal life.

The cross

Our salvation was won for us by Jesus's death on the cross. You were baptized into Christ's whole life, death, and resurrection. We are grateful to him for this gift. We are forever united to him. His sufferings give us courage to live as he did. This is why you were marked by the sign of the cross at your Baptism.

The candle

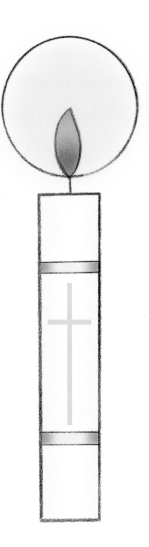

Just as your birthday candles celebrate your birth, your baptismal candle celebrates your birth into God's life. At Baptism there are two types of candles. One candle is the Easter candle. It is used first at the Easter vigil and represents the light of Christ and that Jesus rose from the dead. The other type is the candle your godparent held for you at your Baptism. After you were baptized with the water, your candle was lit from the flame of the Easter candle. Now that you are baptized, you have the light of Jesus within you. Just as Jesus is light for the world, you are called to shine as a light for other people. You are also called to bring light to the world. You can do this by sharing, by telling the truth, by helping others, by praying, and by following Jesus.

The oil

In the Bible, holy oil was used to mark or anoint priests, prophets, and kings. Jesus was anointed by God as priest, prophet, and king. During your Baptism you too were blessed with holy oil. In your own life, you will be like a priest, prophet, and king in following Jesus. You will be like a priest because you will be able to pray for others. You will be like a prophet because you will listen to the word of God and live by it. You will be like a king or queen because you will obey God's rules as Jesus did. Your Baptism made you very special. On the day you were baptized God gave you a special mission to know, love, and praise God and help others to do the same. When you do these things you too are a priest, prophet, and king.

The white garment, baptismal gown

White clothes remind us very much of the Risen Jesus. He is the Lord to whom we belong! The white garment you were given at Baptism shows that you belong to Christ and promise to follow him. In Jesus, the Father adopted you as his child. The color white also symbolizes being clean and pure. The white garment symbolizes that you were cleansed and your sins were washed away. The meaning of the white garment lasts our whole life long. In Baptism we see it as a small white cloth. When someone dies a large white cloth is used at the person's funeral. This white garment reminds us that our baptismal commitment is a covenant we make with God forever.

Stories from the Bible

The Bible Tells Stories About Baptism

Because of your Baptism, you now belong to God's family. How can you know more about this big family? You can read a special, holy book. This book is the Bible. It is the holy word of God. It is like a family photo album, only there are stories instead of pictures. The Bible will tell you about God's love and God's family. Some of the stories will remind you of Baptism!

Lord, your holy word lasts for ever and ever.
Your word is more precious even than gold!
It is sweeter than syrup or the best honey!

(see Psalm 19)

The Bible can teach you many things. It teaches you that God created you and loves you. It teaches you that God will take care of you and never leave you. When you were baptized you became a child of God and a member of the Church. In addition, when you received God's gift of Baptism you received God living inside of you and giving you eternal life. Because the Holy Spirit lives in you, you have the grace to live as God wants you to live.

God Loved Us and Made Our World

At first it was dark, with nothing in sight.
But God was still there! And God called out, "LIGHT!"

Light then appeared, and God went to work.
He made the blue sky, some mud and some dirt.

"I'll fix up the waters just as I please."
So God made the lakes, the rivers and seas.

God wanted green things, so up popped the grass.
He also made trees and shrubs of each class.

"Veggies and flowers that grow will be fine.
I want to have lots, at least ten of each kind."

God made the bright sun. It came out to play.
"Good," God said aloud, "because we have day."

Then God called the stars and moon for the night.
God said again, "Good, now this looks just right!"

God made birds and fish, animals galore.
But God didn't stop. There was one thing more.

"These next special ones my image will bear.
I'll make man and woman. They'll be quite a pair!"

God rested at last. The work had been fun.
"It's all very good. For now I am done."

Did you know?

At the beginning of creation, it was dark. Then God brought the world out of darkness into light. At Baptism you too were brought into God's wonderful light in Christ.

At creation God's spirit breathed upon the waters. At Baptism, the Spirit breathed new life into you.

At creation, God made everything and made it beautiful. At Baptism, you were redeemed by God's Son. You were made a new creation, too!

Noah's Big, Big Boat

One day long ago God looked all around
For one good man, until Noah he found.

"Noah, you and your family hear and obey.
The rest of the people just turn away.

"I'm sending a flood with wave upon wave.
You must build a boat so you will be saved."

Then Noah went out and looked for some nails.
Though there was no rain, he knew God never fails!

The boat, called an ark, was built big and wide.
It had to fit two of each creature inside!

Then the rain came down hard, and the sky grew dark.
But Noah's whole family was safe on the ark.

Animals, insects, and birds of each kind
Were safely inside, not one left behind!

The ark floated on through days and through nights,
Surrounded by water and no land in sight.

At last the rain stopped, so out a dove flew
To help find some land to start things anew.

God promised to never again flood the land.
The sign of his promise? A rainbow so grand!

Did you know?

The story of Noah's Ark is a great reminder of your Baptism. Why? In the story, water was a symbol of danger. God is stronger than the water and saved Noah and his family. It is the same for us. In Baptism, we use water to remind us that God is the one who saves us from all dangers. It also reminds us that God washes us clean and gives us a new, special kind of life.

God Sets His People Free at the Red Sea!

To freedom God's chosen people fled,
But Pharaoh wanted them slaves instead.

The king of Egypt would not let them be
Even when God said, "Set my people free!"

God guided his people along the way,
Through fire at night and with cloud by day.

Until—Red Sea before them, army behind—
There was no escape God's people could find.

Then Moses rose up, and in a loud voice,
He said, "Trust in God, and soon we'll rejoice!

"For our awesome God is mighty to save.
So do as I say. Have faith and be brave!"

He turned to the sea, he lifted his arms.
God's power at work saved people from harm.

The Red Sea opened. It split right in two.
A pathway appeared and the people walked through.

God's people escaped up onto the beach,
And safely beyond the Pharaoh's reach.

Then God closed the sea. "Look what God has done!"
The people all cheered the victory he won!

Did you know?

When God's people crossed the Red Sea, God was fulfilling his promise to take care of them always. God also promises to take care of you! At your Baptism, you became God's child. You belong to God. You are one of God's children, and God continues to stay with you and take care of you.

Jesus Is Baptized

A prophet named John would point out the way
For people to turn to God and be saved.

John spoke what was true, his message was clear:
"Prepare the Lord's way! God's kingdom is near.

"The One who is coming is greater than I.
He is the Messiah, the One from on high."

"But aren't you the one?" the people would ask.
John answered them, "No, that is not my task."

John knew that his work was to help them prepare
Their hearts for the love and life God would share.

John went to the river again and again.
He baptized with water, to cleanse them from sin.

Then one sunny day Jesus came to the shore,
And John felt more certain than ever before.

He knew that this Jesus was special indeed.
"It's you who should baptize, instead of me."

But Jesus knelt humbly, as John stood above.
He rose from the water and down came a dove.

Then John heard God's voice. With awe he was seized.
"This is my dear Son. With him I am pleased."

Did you know?

When Jesus was baptized a dove was seen. The dove is a symbol of the Holy Spirit. At your Baptism, you were baptized in the name of the Father, the Son, and the Holy Spirit. You belong to God and to God's family forever. As a child of God, you have many brothers and sisters! God does this out of great love for you.

Jesus and the First Easter

At night in a garden the guards came with spears.
All Jesus's friends ran away in fear.

The guards brought Jesus to the council and judge.
Shouting for death, the crowds would not budge.

Jesus was blameless. He had done no wrong,
But he carried his cross, though the way was long.

He was hung on the cross, while soldiers jeered.
Mother Mary and John, his friend, stood near.

Jesus died that Friday for you and for me.
But that wasn't the end of the story, you see.

On Sunday some women, at first light of day,
Went to see the tomb where his body lay.

They found a surprise early that morn,
The tomb was empty, the body was gone!

Mary Magdalene saw a man with a hoe,
"Where is Jesus?" she asked. "Please tell if you know!"

"Mary," said the man. It was Jesus, she knew!
"Go and tell my friends they will see me too."

Mary ran quickly with good news to spread.
"I've seen Jesus alive, risen as he said!"

Did you know?

Because of your Baptism, you share in all that Jesus experienced in his lifetime. Baptism connects you to Jesus in a very special way. Through Baptism you share in his eternal life because he wants to be close to you.

God Sends the Spirit to Help

It was time for Jesus to go back home,
But he would not leave his friends alone.

Before departing for heaven again,
A most special gift he promised to send.

He said he'd give them a gift from on high,
God's Holy Spirit to teach and to guide.

The disciples were sad to see Jesus go.
What would happen without him? They didn't know.

Together with Mary they waited and prayed.
In an upstairs room they hid and stayed.

They asked God to show them what they should do.
Then they heard a loud sound—like strong wind that blew.

They felt peace as flames of fire appeared
Above each of their heads. They no longer feared.

God's Holy Spirit had come with power!
Trusting in God, they could be more than cowards!

They now had courage to go out and preach
The message of Jesus, and everywhere teach.

They hurried along, not wasting a minute
To share Good News with the world and all in it.

Did you know?

The Holy Spirit is God. At Pentecost, the Holy Spirit came to Mary and to the many of Jesus's disciples and filled them. At your Baptism, the Holy Spirit came and made a home in you. This means that God's Holy Spirit lives in you and wants to be with you all the time. The Holy Spirit is a very special gift. God's Holy Spirit helps you every day. The Holy Spirit helps you to live each day as a child of God. As God's child you can pray, asking God to help you in all things and at all times.

My Prayers

When you pray you can use formal prayers that you have memorized, or you can just talk to God as you would talk to your best friend. Praying is talking to God about what is in your mind and heart.

THE SIGN OF THE CROSS

In the name of the Father, and of the Son, and of the Holy Spirit. Amen.

OUR FATHER

Our Father, who art in heaven,
hallowed be thy name.
Thy kingdom come. Thy will be done
on earth as it is in heaven.
Give us this day our daily bread,
and forgive us our trespasses
as we forgive those who trespass against us.
And lead us not into temptation;
but deliver us from evil. Amen.

MORNING PRAYER

I adore you, my God. I love you with all my heart.
Thank you for having created me and made me a Christian.
Thank you for having kept me safe this night.
Today I want to please you, Lord. I want to be all yours.
Keep me from sin, Jesus.
Bless everyone in my family. Bless all my friends. Amen.

HAIL MARY

Hail, Mary, full of grace, the Lord is with you.
Blessed are you among women and blessed is the fruit
of your womb, Jesus. Holy Mary, Mother of God, pray
for us sinners, now and at the hour of our death. Amen.

GLORY

Glory to the Father, and to the Son, and
to the Holy Spirit: as it was in the beginning,
is now, and will be forever. Amen.

ANGEL OF GOD

Angel of God, my guardian dear,
to whom God's love entrusts me here;
ever this day be at my side,
to light and guard,
to rule and guide. Amen.

I believe in God,
the Father almighty,
Creator of heaven and earth,
and in Jesus Christ, his only Son, our Lord,
who was conceived by the Holy Spirit,
born of the Virgin Mary,
suffered under Pontius Pilate,
was crucified, died, and was buried;
he descended into hell;
on the third day he rose again from the dead;
he ascended into heaven,
and is seated at the right hand of God
    the Father almighty;
from there he will come again
    to judge the living
    and the dead.
I believe in the Holy Spirit,
the holy catholic Church,
the communion of saints,
the forgiveness of sins,
the resurrection of the body,
and life everlasting. Amen.

Act of Faith

My God, I firmly believe that you are one God in three divine Persons, Father, Son, and Holy Spirit. I believe that your divine Son became man and died for our sins, and that he will come to judge the living and the dead. I believe these and all the truths which the holy Catholic Church teaches, because you have revealed them, who can neither deceive nor be deceived. Amen.

Act of Hope

My God, relying on your infinite goodness and promises, I hope to obtain pardon of my sins, the help of your grace, and life everlasting, through the merits of Jesus Christ, my Lord and redeemer. Amen.

Act of Love

My God, I love you above all things, with my whole heart and soul, because you are all good and worthy of all love. I love my neighbor as myself for the love of you. I forgive all who have injured me, and I ask pardon of all whom I have injured. Amen.

Act of Contrition

My God, I am sorry for my sins with all my heart. In choosing to do wrong and failing to do good, I have sinned against you whom I should love above all things. I firmly intend, with your help, to do penance, to sin no more, and to avoid whatever leads me to sin. Our Savior Jesus Christ suffered and died for us. In his name, my God, have mercy. Amen.

Blessing Before Meals

Bless us, O Lord, and these your gifts, which we are about to receive from your bounty, through Christ our Lord. Amen.

Blessing After Meals

We give you thanks for all your benefits, Almighty God, who live and reign forever. Amen.

Night Prayers

I adore you, my God. I love you with all my heart.
Thank you for the good things you helped me to do today!
(Remember some of these good things.) I may have done some wrong things, too. I am sorry for them. I know that you forgive me. Take care of me while I sleep, Lord.
Please bless me and all those I love. Amen.

Amen
Amen
Amen
Amen
Amen
Amen
AMEN
Amen

Amen

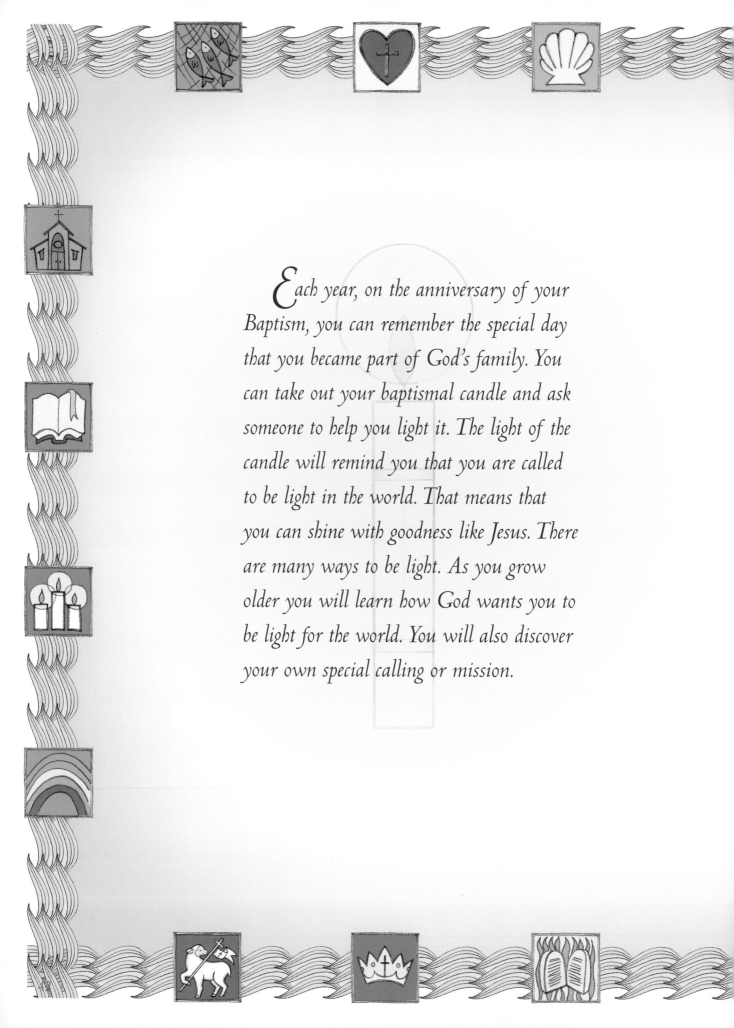

*E*ach year, on the anniversary of your Baptism, you can remember the special day that you became part of God's family. You can take out your baptismal candle and ask someone to help you light it. The light of the candle will remind you that you are called to be light in the world. That means that you can shine with goodness like Jesus. There are many ways to be light. As you grow older you will learn how God wants you to be light for the world. You will also discover your own special calling or mission.

Growing Up

Prayer Service to Celebrate the Anniversary of Your Baptism

You and your family can celebrate the anniversary of your Baptism. You might like to do this before or after a meal. Light your baptismal candle or a special candle during this time of prayer.

A prayer

Dear God, thank you for making me part of your family. Thank you for loving me and watching over me.

The light of this candle reminds me, and all of us here, to be light in the world. Like Jesus we can be patient, we can forgive, and we can be merciful. May every member of our family grow to be more like Jesus, your Son. Amen.

Write your own prayer here

Family or friends can write a prayer here

_____

_____

_____

_____

_____

Together . . .
we pray the prayer that Jesus taught us

As a family you can pray the Our Father together. It is found on page 36.

Did you know?

Each year, all of us in God's family remember our Baptism. We remember it in a special way on the night of Holy Saturday, the day before Easter Sunday. Two of the symbols used for this celebration are candles and water. These remind us that we have been baptized into Christ. They remind us that our sins have been forgiven. We also remember that we are part of God's family!

My Sacramental Record

My First Penance and Reconciliation

_____
(date and Church)

What I remember of this day

_____

_____

_____

My First Communion

_____
(date and Church)

What I remember of this day

_____

_____

_____

My Confirmation

_____
(date and Church)

What I remember of this day

_____

_____

_____

At home, in school, and with my friends, I continue to grow in the life of Jesus

⚜ First Grade ⚜

School _____

Teacher _____

Friends _____

Favorite subjects _____

Favorite things _____

Ways I am growing in Christ _____

⚜ Second Grade ⚜

School _____

Teacher _____

Friends _____

Favorite subjects _____

Favorite things _____

Ways I am growing in Christ _____

Third Grade

School _____

Teacher _____

Friends _____

Favorite subjects _____

Favorite things _____

Ways I am growing in Christ _____

_____

Fourth Grade

School _____

Teacher _____

Friends _____

Favorite subjects _____

Favorite things _____

Ways I am growing in Christ _____

_____

Fifth Grade

School _____

Teacher _____

Friends _____

Favorite subjects _____

Favorite things _____

Ways I am growing in Christ _____

_____

Sixth Grade

School _____

Teacher _____

Friends _____

Favorite subjects _____

Favorite things _____

Ways I am growing in Christ _____

_____

Seventh Grade

School _____

Teacher _____

Friends _____

Favorite subjects _____

Favorite things _____

Ways I am growing in Christ _____

_____

Eighth Grade

School _____

Teacher _____

Friends _____

Favorite subjects _____

Favorite things _____

Ways I am growing in Christ _____

_____

God loves you very much. He wants you to love him, to love others, and to be happy.

God has given each person a mission, a calling. Following God's call for you is a way that you can love others and love God. How do you think God is calling you to serve him when you grow up?

I think God wants me
to serve him and others by

There are so many different ways to serve God. In whatever you do now or when you are older, you are always God's beloved child.

The Daughters of St. Paul operate book and media centers at the following addresses. Visit, call, or write the one nearest you today, or find us at www.pauline.org.

CALIFORNIA
3908 Sepulveda Blvd, Culver City, CA 90230   310-397-8676
935 Brewster Avenue, Redwood City, CA 94063   650-369-4230
5945 Balboa Avenue, San Diego, CA 92111   858-565-9181

FLORIDA
145 SW 107th Avenue, Miami, FL 33174   305-559-6715

HAWAII
1143 Bishop Street, Honolulu, HI 96813   808-521-2731
Neighbor Islands call: 866-521-2731

ILLINOIS
172 North Michigan Avenue, Chicago, IL 60601   312-346-4228

LOUISIANA
4403 Veterans Memorial Blvd, Metairie, LA 70006   504-887-7631

MASSACHUSETTS
885 Providence Hwy, Dedham, MA 02026   781-326-5385

MISSOURI
9804 Watson Road, St. Louis, MO 63126   314-965-3512

NEW YORK
64 West 38th Street, New York, NY 10018   212-754-1110

PENNSYLVANIA
Philadelphia—relocating   215-676-9494

SOUTH CAROLINA
243 King Street, Charleston, SC 29401   843-577-0175

VIRGINIA
1025 King Street, Alexandria, VA 22314   703-549-3806

CANADA
3022 Dufferin Street, Toronto, ON M6B 3T5   416-781-9131